Hammersmith Bridge, July 1827

Hammersmith Bridge was the first suspension bridge over the Thames. It was designed by an engineer, William Tierney Clark, and was opened on 6th October 1827. It was freed from toll in 1880, and demolished four years later when the present bridge was built.

Lithograph by Charles King of Mortlake (1772–1856).

The Garden Front of Barn Elms, 1936

Barn Elms was the home of the Ranelagh Club from 1884 to 1939. The central portion was built by Richard Cartwright in 1694, and the wings were added by Sir Richard Hoare in 1771. It was demolished in 1954, and the estate is now used as school playing-fields.

Pen and ink drawing by Hanslip Fletcher (1874–1955).
Copyright: Times Newspapers Ltd.

GLIMPSES OF
OLD BARNES AND MORTLAKE

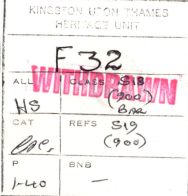

Fairfax House, Mortlake, 1847

This house had a stone fireplace and panelling dated 1620. It stood on the west side of Ship Lane, and was destroyed by fire in 1881. A new house was built on the site, now likewise demolished. The Ship Inn is seen beyond.

Engraving by P. Thompson after C. Pyne.

Published by Hendon Publishing Co. Ltd., Hendon Mill, Nelson, Lancashire.
Text © Barnes & Mortlake History Society, 1984
Printed by Fretwell & Brian Ltd., Goulbourne Street, Keighley, West Yorkshire.

The River at Barn Elms, 1785

The meadows at Barn Elms were a favourite resort for Londoners enjoying a river outing in the 17th and 18th centuries. Pepys records parties here. The bridge indicates the mouth of the Beverley Brook. Engraving by S. Middiman after E. Edwards of Roehampton (1738–1806).

The Castelnau Villas, Barnes, 1842
Nineteen pairs of villas were built on the approach road to Hammersmith Bridge on the initiative of Major C. L. Boileau, who lived in one of them. The name of the road was changed from Bridge Road to Castelnau in 1896.
Engraving by B. R. Davies from design by H. Laxton.
Reproduced by kind permission of the Archives Department of the London Borough of Lambeth.

Rocks Lane, Barnes, c.1820
Rocks Lane became part of the approach road to the new Hammersmith Bridge in 1827. This picture shows the bridge over the Beverley Brook, the gate on to the common and the windmill on Mill Hill.

Wash drawing by James Bourne (1773–1854).

Reproduced by kind permission of Mr David Gould.

The Windmill, Barnes Common, 1780

The land at Mill Hill, originally part of the manorial waste, was enclosed in 1731, and a post mill erected. It was overturned by a violent hurricane on 15th October 1780, and replaced by a smock mill, which stood until 1836.

Outline drawing by E. Edwards of Roehampton (1738–1806).

The Old Workhouse, Barnes, 1885

The inhabitants of Barnes subscribed towards the building of a workhouse in 1778 on 23 acres of common between Queen's Ride and Upper Richmond Road. The architect was Kenton Couse. The building became a private house in 1836. It was demolished in 1961, and flats now occupy the site.

Engraving by Clough Bromley (1850–c.1904).

Brass of William Millebourne, 1415
Brass of Rev. Nicholas Clerk, 1480

The Millebourne brass disappeared from St. Mary's Church about 1787. That of Clerk, who was Rector of Barnes 1477–1480, disappeared later, possibly about 1852. It was given to St. Peter's Church, Clapham in 1912, but it was not identified until 1973.

St. Mary's Church, Barnes, 1837

This south view shows the original 12th- and 13th-century church and the late 15th-century tower. An aisle was added on the north side in the 18th century. The church was gutted by fire in 1978, and reopened in 1984.

Lithograph by Laura Jones.

Scene on Barnes Terrace, c.1800

The scene is set where the High Street joins the Terrace. Several of the houses are clearly recognizable today. The White Hart Inn can be seen at the far end, and beyond it Castelnau House, Mortlake, in a break in the trees.

Watercolour by T. Rowlandson (1756–1827).

Barnes Terrace, 1823

This view is from the White Hart, and features in the foreground No. 28 (d'Antraigues) which still stands. Beyond the trees of Elm Bank and more houses on the Terrace can be seen Waring's Brewery and the garden wall of St. Ann's.
Lithograph by W. Westall (1781–1850).

Suthrey House, Mortlake, c.1832

This ancient house was the home of the King family in the early 19th century. The artist's wife is at the window and their children, Mary Ann and Charles, are in the garden near the river. Wilfred Scawen Blunt, poet and traveller, lived here as a boy in 1853.

Watercolour by Charles King of Mortlake (1772–1856).

Reproduced by kind permission of the owner.

The Queen's Head, Mortlake, c.1875

The inn was rebuilt about 1885, and closed to customers in 1952. The neglected building on the left stood on the site of the tapestry works, and was demolished in 1951. Its site is now an open space.

Lithograph by Albert Betts of Mortlake (1836–1906).

Eton and Westminster Boat Race, 1843

The match was rowed from Putney to Mortlake on 1st August 1843, and Eton won by 14 lengths. The picture is noteworthy for its excellent detail of the buildings on the Mortlake riverside from the church to Bulls Alley.

Lithograph by R. H. Thomas (1816–1884).

Barnes Terrace   Malt House   Barnes Terrace

Barne.

This view forms part of a panorama over 55 feet in length,

Aquatint from *The Panorama of the Thames*

ce, 1829
rides a unique record of all buildings visible from the river.
ndon to Richmond, published by Samuel Leigh.

St. Mary's Church, Mortlake, 1750
The earliest view of the church. It shows the tower and nave of 1543, and the 17th-century Vestry House is seen behind the watch house on the left. The Queen's Head inn sign is suspended across the High Street.

Engraving by J. Roberts after J. B. C. Chatelain (1710–1771).

St. Mary's Church, Mortlake, c.1805

The viewpoint most favoured by artists. The south aisle was built in 1725, and was replaced in 1840. The top storey of the tower had recently been refaced in brick, and the battlements removed. The cupola and clock were added early in the 18th century.

Watercolour by H. Petrie (1768–1842).

Reproduced by kind permission of the Archives Department of the London Borough of Lambeth.

East Sheen Chapel, c.1840

This chapel was built in 1716 for the congregation which was described as 'Presbyterian and Independent'. It later became Congregational, and ceased to be so used in 1900, but the building can still be identified at the corner of South Worple Way and Sheen Lane.

Engraving by H. A. Ogg of Mortlake after J. Cullum.

Thames Bank, Mortlake, c.1850
The high-pitched roof of Thames Cottage (formerly church property) can be seen beyond the Ship Inn, and further on is the summer-house, which appears more prominently in the next picture.
Oil painting by F. W. Watts (1800–1862).

Thames Bank, Mortlake, 1824

The picturesque gazebo or summer-house on the wall of Old Cromwell House was a prominent feature of the riverside until its demolition about 1855. In the distance Castelnau House is seen in the trees.

Oil painting by W. H. Harriott of Mortlake (1780–1839).

Reproduced by kind permission of the owner.

Cromwell House, Mortlake, 1918

A new Cromwell House was built by James Wigan on Thames Bank between Leyden House and Riverside House on his marriage in 1858, and later enlarged. The family lived there until 1919. The house was demolished in 1947.

Watercolour by Miss Maud Randall of Barnes.
Reproduced by kind permission of the owner.

Houses at Priests Bridge, 1893

The name for the crossing here of the Beverley Brook dates from the Middle Ages. It is thought to relate to the use of the bridge by priests travelling between Mortlake and Wimbledon. This stretch of road was by-passed to the south in 1929.

Drawing by Albert Betts of Mortlake (1836–1906).

The Bull Inn, East Sheen, 1903

The inn formed the centre of Clarence Row, which was built in 1792 by J. C. Halford, the owner of Mortlake Brewery. He named it in honour of the Duke of Clarence, who was living nearby at Clarence Lodge, Priory Lane. The inn was rebuilt in 1938.

Pen and wash drawing by W. L. Turner of East Sheen (1866–1920).

Sheen House, East Sheen, 1808

The house was rebuilt in 1788 by Charles Bowles, glass manufacturer. He was succeeded in 1806 by the banker, Henry Hope. The west end of Shrewsbury Avenue marks the site of the house, which was demolished in 1907. The grounds extended the length of Richmond Park Road.

Temple Grove, East Sheen, 1800

The east front of the house facing Sheen Lane, believed to date from 1611. It was demolished by Sir Thomas Bernard in 1808. His rebuilding disappeared a century later, when Palmerston Road and Observatory Road were constructed.

Engraving by J. P. Malcolm (1767–1815).

East Sheen Lodge, 1889

This view dates from the marriage of the Earl of Fife, who had lived here since 1880, with Princess Louise of Wales. It shows the south front of the house, which was demolished in 1965. It stood on the north side of York Avenue, with grounds extending to Richmond Park.

Engraving by G. Montbard, i.e. C. A. Loye (1841–1905).

Blind Lane, East Sheen, c.1895

A view taken from the top of Blind Lane (renamed Temple Sheen Road in 1909) across market gardens, now the site of Coval Road and Medcroft Gardens, to Mortlake Brewery beyond.
Drawing by Albert Betts of Mortlake (1836–1906).

Sheen Gate, Richmond Park, c.1895
The gate at East Sheen was one of the original gates provided by Charles I across an old highway at this point. The lodge shown here was rebuilt about 1910, and the gate was replaced in 1926.
Drawing by Albert Betts of Mortlake (1836–1906).

Sheen Lodge, Richmond Park, c.1860

This thatched house, later called Sheen Cottage, was built in the line of the Park wall to the east of Sheen Gate in the 18th century. For well over a century it was the home successively of the Adam family and Sir Richard Owen, the naturalist. It was destroyed by enemy action in 1944, and never rebuilt.

Lithograph by Day & Son after J. Erxleben.

Bog Lodge, Richmond Park, 1823

Bog Lodge is the oldest house in the Park, being in existence when the Park was enclosed in 1637, but it was largely rebuilt in the 18th century. It was for long the home of successive head keepers. This view outlines the dome of St. Paul's Cathedral on the horizon.

Pencil drawing by S. de Koster (1767–1831).